Pathways to Play!

Combining Sensory Integration and Integrated Play Groups

Theme-Based Activities for Children
with Autism Spectrum and Other Sensory-Processing Disorders

Pathways to Play!

Combining Sensory Integration and Integrated Play Groups

Theme-Based Activities for Children
with Autism Spectrum and Other Sensory-Processing Disorders

Glenda Fuge, M.S., OTR/L
Rebecca Berry, M.S., PT

Foreword by Lorna Jean King

Autism Asperger Publishing Co.
P.O. Box 23173
Shawnee Mission, KS 66283-0173
www.asperger.net

© 2004 by Autism Asperger Publishing Company
P.O. Box 23173
Shawnee Mission, KS 66283-0173
www.asperger.net

Publisher's Cataloging-in-Publication
(Provided by Quality Books, Inc.)

Fuge, Glenda.
      Pathways to play! : combining sensory integration and integrated play groups : theme-based activities for children with autism spectrum and other sensory-processing disorders / by Glenda Fuge, Rebecca Berry.
      p. cm.
      Includes bibliographical references.
      Library of Congress Control Number: 2004101470
      ISBN 1-931282-55-2

      1. Autism in children--Treatment. 2. Play therapy. 3. Sensorimotor integration. I. Berry, Rebecca, 1961- II. Title.

This book is designed in Helvetica Neue and Spumoni

Managing Editor: Kirsten McBride
Editorial Support: Ginny Biddulph

Printed in Korea

ACKNOWLEDGMENTS

The completion of this manual represents a collaboration with numerous friends that could never have been foreseen a few years ago. Many have given their time, effort, and love to support the therapy model used at Developmental Pathways for Kids. We want to express heartfelt thanks to all of those who participated in this project and gave us support as we traveled down the pathways to play.

Thank you to:

Pamela Wolfberg, who provided the Integrated Play Groups model and offered generous and insightful suggestions regarding this manual.

The faculty and principal at Redeemer School, who embraced our vision and shared their students in our program.

All the children at Redeemer Lutheran School, who participated as expert players and joyfully used their hearts and hands in thousands of play sessions.

Rosemary Behrens for technical support, patience, and diligence.

Erin Sarpa for her creative design expertise and willingness to take on an "extra" job.

The many novice players who have helped us expand our knowledge and expertise.

And special thanks to our families, who have been our most faithful supporters!

– Glenda Fuge
– Rebecca Berry

TABLE OF CONTENTS

Appendices

References and Suggested Readings

FOREWORD

By writing this manual, Glenda Fuge and Rebecca Berry have done a great service for parents, teachers, occupational, physical and speech-language therapists, and anybody else who is working to improve the quality of life for children, both in the present and in their future lives. The authors combine their expertise in occupational and physical therapy with extensive experience in working with children in their therapy center, Developmental Pathways for Kids.

A widely accepted goal for children with special needs is that they be integrated into community institutions as fully as possible. For children, the major community institution is the school, whether it be public, charter, or private. The problem is that until now, no one has provided the bricks and mortar, the actual methods of integrating the vital part of the child's life – the relationships with other children – the social fabric of the child's life.

Fuge and Berry have taken the vague and fuzzy concepts of integration and given them form and substance by providing guidelines and specific methods for melding children with special needs and typically developing children into happy and cohesive play groups.

The themed activities described here will provide a springboard for the imaginations of group facilitators and the children themselves. The children will embellish the ideas presented and be a constant source of new activities. The "facilitator prompts" will empower even the most inexperienced teacher or parent to get started. The children will do the rest.

An integral component of successful play groups is the adult facilitator's understanding of how children develop competency in sensory-motor activities. Fuge and Berry have done an admirable job of explaining briefly the principles of sensory integration and relating them to specific plans for children's play. The wonderful thing is that activities that are vital to the children with special needs also enhance the capabilities of the typical children. Everyone benefits.

It is exciting to know that parents, teachers and therapists now have a valuable guide to enhance the development and the happiness of so many children. It is remarkable resource. Well done, Glenda and Rebecca!!

    Lorna Jean King, OTR/L, FAOTA
    Director Emeritus
    The Children's Center for Neurodevelopmental Studies
    Glendale, Arizona

INTRODUCTION

This manual provides ideas for working with children on the autism spectrum. In addition to parents and teachers, it is designed to be used as a tool for pediatric occupational therapists, physical therapists, and speech and language pathologists interested in providing structured peer play activities with a sensory-motor foundation.

All play activities are based on an innovative program developed by the authors at Developmental Pathways for Kids, a pediatric therapy clinic in Redwood City, California (see Appendix A). This program combines sensory integration (described on pp. 1-13) and the Integrated Play Groups model, a peer play intervention originated by Pamela Wolfberg, author of, among others, *Peer Play and the Autism Spectrum: The Art of Guiding Children's Socialization and Imagination* (Shawnee Mission, KS: Autism Asperger Publishing Co., 2003) (see Appendix B). By utilizing sensory-integration strategies within an Integrated Play Groups format, a balanced partnership is created. Using principles of sensory integration and including typical peers as "expert players" in facilitated play groups is important when working with children within the autism spectrum as it helps to:
- build circles of communication and social language skills
- work on functional IEP goals
- generalize skills across environments
- document social/play skill progress in a peer setting
- maximize mainstreaming opportunities

The theme-based activities presented in this manual provide opportunities to build social communication skills, peer interaction skills, and sensory-motor skills while diversifying a child's repertoire of play. When children participate in activities that are intrinsically motivating, learning naturally occurs. Specifically, within Integrated Play Groups, successful therapy and play sessions must build on activities of interest to the novice player and also capture the novice player's attention. When selecting from the following activities, these considerations must be kept in mind, given the individual children you are working with.

All play themes and activities are arranged in an easy-to-use format, including
- facilitator prompts
- a materials list
- listing of the developmental foundations addressed in a given play activity
- a worksheet page for each play theme for making notes and observations

To create a background for the 40 activities, the following section provides information about sensory integration and the difficulties often experienced in this area by individuals with autism spectrum disorders.

SENSORY INTEGRATION

Sensory integration refers to the organization of sensation for adaptive use. When a person uses his or her body and the environment in a creative or useful way, the result is called an adaptive response. For example, a child seated on a swing on the playground receives information from muscles, joints, and the vestibular system (the inner-ear mechanisms that give us a sense of movement and gravity) that allows her to maintain balance and coordination and successfully pump on the swing. A well-organized adaptive motor response results in further integration of sensations that arise from that response. As a result, with practice and repetition on the swing, the child receives more information about how her body relates in space and further refines balance and coordination skills. The child's nervous system eventually becomes able to generalize skills and allow the child to participate effectively on a variety of moving equipment activities. When sensory integration is efficient and effective, it leads the central nervous system to a more organized state for optimal self-calming, attention, and learning (Kranowitz, 1998). The activities presented in this book will help ensure such a state, with special focus on children on the autism spectrum.

Although all children are born with the capacity for sensory integration, they must develop it further by interacting with their environment and making adaptive responses (Ayres, 1979). For example, a toddler learning to walk maintains an immature upright position with a wide base of support; that is, he stands with his feet wide apart and knees slightly bent and holds his hands in an upright "high-guard" position. With practice, the child becomes adept at maneuvering through the environment and, therefore, becomes less reliant on an immature posture for successful walking.

Modulation

An important aspect of sensory integration is modulation. When we demonstrate modulation, there is a balance between our level of arousal and the intensity of the stimulation we are experiencing. This is viewed as the body's internal thermostat, which gives us the ability to become alert or calm as appropriate for a given situation. When a child has sensory-integrative problems, he does not have this internal capacity to modulate the level of arousal (Reisman & King, 1993). For example, in the over-responsive or hypersensitive child, the nervous system is processing information from the environment inaccurately and, as a result, the child's responses are inaccurate. The over-aroused child may be unable to screen out irrelevant information from the environment because his nervous system is registering all the information it receives and is paying attention to each and every stimulus. For example, his attention may be averted by noises in the room (a fan blowing), overhead lights, or a wide variety of visual information (for example, a bright, cluttered bulletin board). Not surprisingly, this child may be unable to stay seated and focus on a board game with peers because he cannot screen out the background noise, lights, or visual field.

Conversely, if a child is under-aroused, she may not be able to maintain attention during circle time. Since this child has a nervous system that is under-responsive to sensory stimulation, she may require intense stimulation to register a response. Her nervous system is not registering information correctly from the environment, so her responses are inaccurate. This child may appear lethargic, withdrawn or passive. Without increased information or sensory input (loud music, movement, attractive visual prompts) during circle time, this child may not be able to sustain sufficient focus to participate.

Sensory-Integration Therapy

Therapy based on sensory-integration theory, which is the foundation for the activities presented in this book, focuses on tactile, vestibular, proprioceptive, and visual-sensory input, as well as the auditory, gustatory, and olfactory systems (see pp. 3-12). That is, therapy is directed at normalizing the child's responses to sensory input and developing more adaptive and functional motor skills. A major premise of sensory-integrative therapy is that movement activities should be self-initiated to elicit adaptive responses. Therapy is thought to be most effective when the child is motivated and having fun. In childhood, play is the medium through which therapy is adapted (DeGangi, 2000). Therefore, sensory-integration activities are carefully chosen so as best to match a child's developmental level, motor competency, and sensory-processing style to support play experiences.

The sensory systems (tactile, vestibular, proprioceptive, auditory, visual, olfactory, and gustatory) are the foundation or "base" for sensory-motor, perceptual-motor and cognitive skill development. Thus, accurate perception and registration of sensory input in each system is required for successful development. Children on the autism spectrum often display an imbalance within one or more foundational systems that impact the development of higher-level skills. Dysfunction in sensory integration, for example, occurs when the brain is inefficiently processing sensory input from the body and the environment. As a result of inaccurate sensory registration, the child has difficulty making an adaptive or functional response to sensations encountered in everyday life. A child who is over-responsive or hypersensitive to tactile input may be upset by the feeling of the tag in the back of his shirt, for example. Other children who are hyporesponsive may not notice that their pants are on backwards. Both types of children are processing tactile input inaccurately, which, in turn, impacts their eye-hand coordination, fine-motor skills, force or grading of movement, motor planning, as well as higher-level skills such as self-regulation, self-esteem, and social skills (Ayres, 1979).

In the following, we will take a brief look at the various senses along with examples of how difficulties in each area can impact a child's development and daily functioning.

Tactile System

The tactile system involves the ability to receive and interpret sensation and stimuli through contact with the skin. The tactile system is the primary sensory system at birth and remains critical throughout life. It consists of two discrete tracts: the protective (flight-fright-or-fight response) and the discriminative (information about people and objects in the environment). Thus, a baby is born with both the defensive tactile sense for survival and the discriminative sense for learning about the environment. At birth, the defensive sense predominates. This system plays an important role in initiating and planning movement and exploring the environment. Through touch exploration the child learns how his body relates to others and the environment and learns how to grade (adjust) movement and force for effective skill mastery. As the child matures, the discriminative sense takes precedence in most activities of everyday life, including dressing, eating, and playing. The more a child explores through touch and movement, the more efficient he becomes at mastering age-appropriate skills. Mastery of age-appropriate skills develops when sensations are integrated and registered for functional outputs. For example, the child learns through touch how much force to apply to grasp a hanging toy and bring it to his mouth.

Tactile Discrimination

The ability to discriminate tactile information is important to be able to locate touch on the body and gives us the ability to register both sensations when two places have been simultaneously touched, for example. In addition, the discriminative sense helps the child understand that individual body parts contribute to the whole (integrated body scheme). Fine-motor skills are often compromised in the child with poor tactile discrimination. Since this child's tactile system is not accurately registering information, spacing, letter formation, motor accuracy with tools, and grading of force are negatively affected. For example, in order to calculate how hard to press down a pencil while writing, the child must be able to use sufficient pressure to mark the paper without pressing so hard that the paper tears (Haron & Henderson, 1985).

Touch combined with movement allows tactile discrimination to occur, which is an important aspect of motor planning (Haron & Henderson, 1985) because the two systems work together to give more information to the brain about how the body relates to others and to objects in the environment. For example, a child standing on a textured balance board gets information from both his tactile system (touch) and his vestibular system (movement), and this multisensory input helps him to balance.

The ability to tolerate touch experiences is one of the early aspects of developing self-regulation (homeostasis), which allows the child to explore the environment in a more meaningful way. When the tactile input is out of balance, exploration is limited, which prevents the child from using her sense of touch in conjunction with other senses to give meaning to how her body and the environment interact. As we have mentioned, reactions to touch input can range from over-responsiveness (defensiveness) to under-responsiveness (Fisher & Dunn, 1983). A child who seems to be unaware of touch (under-responsive) does not react to intense pain, bites or hits herself, or is unaware of messiness on her face. Such a child may also be described as hyposensitive to tactile input (DeGangi, 2000).

Protective Tactile System

The protective tactile system is activated by light touch, skin temperature changes, vibration, and pressure. It is designed to trigger the flight-fright-or-fight response when we perceive we are in danger. When this system is hyper-reactive, we may say that the threshold is too low and is, therefore, defensive (Mailloux, 1992). With increased arousal comes an increased reaction and sensitivity to all other sensory input. For example, a child who negatively responds to light touch from a peer brushing up against him in line may react to this input by pushing the peer (a protective reaction). This child may remain in that "protective state" for the rest of the day, making other activities unduly difficult.

Special Difficulties for Children with Autism Spectrum Disorders

Children on the autism spectrum often display tactile defensiveness resulting in refusal to participate in play activities such as "messy" art projects involving a variety of textures or maintaining close proximity to peers (Baraneck, Foster, & Berkson, 1997). Conversely, some children are hyposensitive to touch and may not react to pain or demonstrate self-injurious behaviors (head banging, biting, and pinching).

Vestibular System

The vestibular system develops early so that the growing fetus and infant can receive and respond to specific movement stimuli. Thus, it is important because it allows the infant to orient in space and plays a role in exploring the environment and developing early adaptive movements. It has a profound effect on play that includes movement, such as games that require the ability to stand on one foot and maintain balance (kicking a ball).

The vestibular system regulates our sense of movement and gravity. Information is received by mechanisms in the inner ear and is passed through a complicated network of connections to other areas of the brain. According to Ayres (1979), "The vestibular system is the unifying system. All other types of sensation are processed in reference to this basic vestibular information. Input from the vestibular system provides a basic framework for other aspects of our experiences" (pp. 70-71). By registering and responding to the pull of gravity, stimulation to the inner ear provides information about balance and movement. Movements initiated by the vestibular system influence muscle tone, equilibrium, visual tracking, arousal, spatial awareness (body in space), and behavior through complex interactions of the nervous system (Fisher, 1991). A child with a poorly developed vestibular system can be described as having low muscle tone. Such a child may appear floppy, may slump in the chair during seated activities, and may fatigue easily with physical exertion.

The vestibular system also has an indirect influence on auditory processing by helping the auditory system attend to sound because of the two structures' close proximity in the brain and complex interactions between them. For example, a child swinging (the swinging movement provides vestibular input to the inner-ear mechanisms) is more likely to achieve and maintain an alert state, which then enhances her ability to receive and respond to auditory input, as when a teacher is giving directions.

The vestibular system responds to the position of the head in relation to gravity and accelerated or decelerated movements. Thus, the system provides gravitational security when moving in space. A secure sense of body-spatial awareness contributes to the development of emotional stability by providing the child with a sense of safety that comes from knowing his feet are firmly planted on the ground (DeGangi, 2000). Children must also have accurate gravitational security to participate in activities with their feet off the ground. The vestibular system gives the child's nervous system information about whether he is moving or not and how fast and in what direction he is moving.

Special Difficulties for Children with Autism Spectrum Disorders

Children who lack adequate vestibular functioning are often insecure in their body movements and fearful of movements in space and may demonstrate emotional insecurity by running away (flight), crying (fright), or fighting with others when asked to participate in movement activities. The child who is hypersensitive to vestibular inputs may have a strong preference for upright postures and demonstrate low muscle tone, slowness in developing motor skills, delayed balance, and/or fear of irregular or unexpected movement (DeGangi & Greenspan, 1988). Some children with autism are hyposensitive to vestibular input and may crave movement activities, becoming upset when restrained from actions such as spinning, twirling, or swinging. Often these children are described as fearless because they constantly test limits, act impulsively, and seem unaware of safety issues (for example, a child who is seeking vestibular input might climb up and jump off of high surfaces unaware of the dangers involved).

Proprioceptive System

The proprioceptive system consists of muscle and joint receptors and various nervous system connections and responds to movement by stretching and bending muscles. During standing and sitting, the muscles and joints consistently send sensory information about the extent of movement, muscle tension, pressure, joint movement, and body position in space to the central nervous system. This, in turn, influences motor planning, spatial awareness and, eventually, behavior.

For example, information from joint receptors in the arm and shoulder (proprioceptors) guides the child's movements so that he can demonstrate mature motor acts, such as throwing a ball to a peer. The proprioceptive input from the receptors in the muscles and joints surrounding the shoulder gives feedback so the child can demonstrate adequate timing, force, sequencing, and visual-motor integration during a ball throw game with a peer. Finally, successful participation in the activity gives the child's nervous system feedback to refine his skill.

The proprioceptive system develops through weight bearing and movement against gravity. Hence the system is critical in the maturation of reflexes and development of equilibrium and balance reactions. For example, a child crawling through a darkened tunnel uses proprioceptive rather than vision input to guide movement. Deep pressure is provided to the muscles and joints as the child crawls through the tunnel, which helps to define where the child's body is in space and, in turn, helps to guide and direct her movements.

The proprioceptive system develops together with the tactile and vestibular systems. They work together through a complex feedback/feed-forward system to enhance the development of postural control, balance, sequencing and coordination of movement (DeGangi, 2000). For example, the child's ability to sit on a swing and throw a bean bag at a target requires adequate information from both the proprioceptive and the visual system.

The proprioceptive system influences arousal states by modulating the vestibular and tactile systems. That is, it calms the nervous system by providing an overriding input that can inhibit tactile or vestibular information from interfering with participation in activities. For example, deep pressure is a therapeutic strategy used to reduce sensory defensiveness over time (Ayres & Tickle, 1980). When a child participates in activities that provide active resistance (traction or pulling of the muscles or joints) or compression to muscles and joints prior to a messy art activity, the child is better able to tolerate or inhibit a flight-or-fright response.

Visual feedback supports the proprioceptive system by providing information about posture and movement. Thus, it gives additional information to support body-spatial awareness to monitor posture and motor accuracy. By comparing how something feels to how it looks, the child develops visual perception (the way we make sense of what we see). A child standing on a moving platform swing gets input through his muscles and joints so that he can feel how his body moves on the swing. Additionally, he uses his vision to gain feedback about where he is in space and assist with postural control. In short, the visual input combined with proprioceptive input allows the child to make sense of what he is feeling and at the same time maintain his balance on the moving swing.

Special Difficulties for Children with Autism Spectrum Disorders

Children on the autism spectrum are often described by their parents as "crashers and bangers"; that is, they are trying to self-regulate by giving themselves deep pressure for calming. An environment that is rich in proprioceptive opportunities such as tug of war, hanging from a trapeze, pushing a heavy ball, or jumping on a trampoline, promotes a calmer, less reactive child, who will be better able to participate in a variety of activities without sensory overload and the need to self-regulate as described above.

Auditory System

The inner ear is comprised of semi-circular canals (dynamic balance structure), cochlea (houses the receptor for hearing), and vestibule (static balance structure). The auditory system responds to vibration, sound, and movement.

Auditory Perception

Auditory perception gives us the ability to receive, identify, discriminate, understand and respond to sounds. Most important, it enables us to interpret or attach meaning to sound. For example, we use auditory perception to attach meaning to the sound of a siren – here comes a fire truck or ambulance.

The auditory system is closely associated with the vestibular system due to their close proximity in the central nervous system. The vestibular system may be stimulated with movement or vibration to improve auditory and language processes (DeGangi, 2000). As a result, many speech pathologists (Ayres, 1982) report an expansion of vocalization when a child is working in a swing because movement in the swing (vestibular input) promotes an alertness and organization of the child's nervous system, which has a positive influence on the child's speech and language systems. Indeed, the movement may promote a readiness for learning by increasing the child's attention.

Auditory Processing

Auditory processing and language skills develop with well-organized vestibular, proprioceptive, and tactile systems (the foundational systems at the lower level of the brain). These foundational systems support interactions with the higher-level brain functions (cognition). When a child's developing nervous system is provided with activities that incorporate opportunities for enhanced sensory intake such as movement with music, sensory-motor, perceptual-motor, and cognitive skills are developed and enhanced. A child with an intact, fully functioning auditory-processing system develops adequate receptive (what we hear) and expressive (what we say) language. Conversely, when a child has difficulty extracting the meaning from hearing spoken language, he may be demonstrating a central auditory-processing disorder.

Special Difficulties for Children with Autism Spectrum Disorders

When auditory processing is poor, a child may have difficulty pronouncing words, hearing in groups, focusing on foreground sounds while blocking out background sounds, remembering and sequencing multistep directions, and following verbal directions (DeGangi, 2000). This may manifest in behavioral reactions, tuning out the environment, frustration, and other reactions.

Visual System

The visual system is comprised of a generalized system and a discriminative system. The generalized system gives us the ability to see (eyesight); it provides the prerequisites for vision (Kranowitz, 1998). The discriminative system gives us information about the physical properties and spatial relationships (perception) about people and objects in the environment. The visual system supports other foundational systems. For example, the visual and vestibular systems work together to provide accurate information about the environment for balance and coordination, enabling a child to swing a bat and hit a target while maintaining his balance.

Color, which has visual appeal, can be used effectively to alter an environment to support modulation and self-regulation (the ability to attain, change and maintain an arousal state in response to changes in the environment). This is important because sustained attention is essential for learning. Some colors are known to be innately alerting visually (magenta and electric blue), others to be calming (yellow, pink, or light blue). In order to process visually, we must first alert to the visual information by directing our eyes to the visual information, filtering out what is important (at the brainstem level) and focusing on the focal field as well as background information.

Special Difficulties for Children with Autism Spectrum Disorders

Children with autism spectrum disorders characteristically avoid eye contact and sometimes use their peripheral vision to observe. Greenspan (1997) postulates that individuals with autism spectrum disorders look out of the corner of their eyes because they are only using one side of their brain, a sign of poor bilateral coordination. Additionally, these children may have difficulty screening out relevant visual information from nonrelevant information and may have poor coordination of the eyes for focused work. Such children may require clear spatial cues in the environment (e.g., a boundary drawn around areas for written work) to avoid becoming overwhelmed by a cluttered room.

Many children on the autism spectrum have difficulties with visual-motor perception, resulting in problems with reading social cues as well as visual-motor coordination. A child with poor visual perception may seem to get "lost in space," lose his way when exiting a familiar classroom if he goes out a different door, etc. Another problem for many children on the autism spectrum is recognition of affective expressions, which relies on integrating auditory and visual-perceptual skills over time and space (DeGangi, 2000). To understand facial expressions a child uses the discriminative visual system to look at the characteristics of the face and auditory input to interpret vocal intonation.

Olfactory System

The olfactory system is comprised of sensory receptors in the nasal passages, which in turn send information to the olfactory bulb located in the midbrain. Smells bypass structures in the midbrain, taking a shortcut to the amygdala (part of the brain responsible for emotional memory). Therefore, smells process faster and have a greater impact (stronger emotional component) than other sensory experiences. Strong-intensity olfactory input stimulates arousal for task involvement and completion. Mild-intensity olfactory input facilitates exploratory behaviors and stimulates naturally occurring activities (Dunn, 1991). For some children, several drops of peppermint on a bean bag that is being tossed between peers can provide intense olfactory input for increased arousal. For others, a small amount of lemon incorporated into shaving cream and a shape sorter may increase motivation to explore with the hands and work with the shape sorter.

Thus, pleasant smells may be combined with positive movement experiences to optimize learning and engagement by providing emotionally positive and successful memories. By using scents that are typically alerting, such as peppermint or lemon, activities can be enhanced for a child who is under-aroused. For a child who is easily over-aroused, scents that are typically calming, such as vanilla or lavender, can be used to help the child stay focused and decrease distractibility. However, it is important to remember that each child is different; a scent that works for one child may not work for another (Higley & Leatham, 1998). As mentioned, typically, an under-aroused child responds with an increased alertness to peppermint scent, but for other children, the peppermint scent may need to be combined with other sensory input for maximum effectiveness.

Special Difficulties for Children with Autism Spectrum Disorders

During play themes involving snacks, some children with autism spectrum disorders avoid the activity (Dunn, 1991) or engage in inappropriate, negative behaviors such as throwing food and/or refusing to sit at the table. These behaviors may be related to poor sensory processing. A child who is overly sensitive (defensive) to certain odors may be unable to control her over-response to the smell of the snack food. When seated with peers at the table, the combination of the close proximity (light, unexpected touch) and the odor (smell) may cause the child to refuse to participate, throw the food, or run away from the table (flight-fright-or-fight response).

Gustatory System

The gustatory system is comprised of taste buds, the tongue, and their neural connections. The sense of taste is strongly related to the touch and smell of stimuli. Thus, when food is placed in the mouth, touch receptors on the tongue and cheeks tell us if the food is bitter, sweet, hot or cold. Food can affect a child's arousal state. For example, a cold popsicle can increase a child's ability to stay alert. Not surprisingly, some children demonstrate oral defensiveness. That is, they dislike or avoid certain textures or types of food. For example, they may be over- or under-sensitive to spicy or hot foods, may avoid putting objects in their mouth, and/or may intensely dislike tooth brushing or face washing.

Special Difficulties for Children with Autism Spectrum Disorders

Children with autism spectrum disorder are often described as "picky eaters." They may demonstrate an increased response to taste and texture of many foods. Some may react defensively to extreme temperatures, preferring foods that are at room temperature. Other children may prefer specific textures, like crunchy chips, to the exclusion of almost all soft, smooth foods (e.g., Jello).

Outcomes of Sensory Processing:
MUSCLE TONE AND MOTOR PLANNING

Two outcomes of sensory processing – muscle tone and motor planning – will be discussed below due to their importance in this context. To some degree, peer play is dependent on a child's muscle tone, gross- and fine-motor skill development, and ability to plan and execute motor acts. For example, the ability to play a kick ball game with a peer requires adequate muscle tone to resist gravity and stand on one foot and kick with the other. Additionally, getting the idea and planning how to kick a ball are essential prior to the actual execution of the kick.

One of the hallmarks of autism spectrum disorders is that many children have sensory-processing disturbances. In these children, some sensory inputs may be "turned on louder," whereas others are significantly "turned down." When there is an imbalance in sensory processing, outputs (muscle tone and motor planning) may be impaired (Siegel, 2003).

Muscle Tone

Muscle tone is the condition in which a muscle at rest is in a steady state of contraction – the ability of a muscle to resist a force for a considerable period of time without a change in length. A child needs adequate muscle tone to sit up and support his head in an upright position against gravity, for example. Muscle tone does not equal function or strength. Instead, it is the resting state of the muscle. Therefore, a child may have low muscle tone and have adequate strength to sit up and walk, yet may not be able to sustain the posture long enough to complete a task.

Muscle tone is the result of the following: (a) adequate stimuli received from numerous receptors in the skin, ligaments, tendons, joint capsules, muscles, and vestibular organs; (b) integration of the sensory signals in the central nervous system; (c) outgoing impulses to muscles; and (d) feedback from receptors. This complex interaction gives a child the ability to sit upright in a chair and sustain this posture over time (endurance), for example.

Special Difficulties for Children with Autism Spectrum Disorders

Low muscle tone may be seen in children with sensory-integration processing problems, including children with autism spectrum disorders. For example, the child may have poor postural control and poor joint stability, resulting in compromised oral-motor control, fine-motor dexterity, gross-motor coordination, and endurance (Ayres, 1979). A child with low muscle tone is described as floppy, weak, tired, unmotivated, lazy or clumsy. During play, children with low muscle tone often tire easily or avoid activities requiring physical exertion (Trott, Laurel, & Windeck, 1993).

Motor Planning

Motor planning (praxis) encompasses the ability to organize a purposeful plan of action. Children who have efficient sensory integration usually have good motor-planning skills. Problems with motor planning are called dyspraxia. A child who has problems with praxis does not see the environment in terms of movement possibilities. For example, children with dyspraxia who confront a new playground structure might run around the structure, stand back and look at it, and finally make purposeless movements instead of climbing on and exploring. Children with developmental dyspraxia lack internal cognitive organization to focus thoughts and actions and are, therefore, often susceptible to distraction (Ayres, 1979).

There are three stages in motor planning: (a) ideation (development of the conceptual organization of skill or task – coming up with an idea of a movement or activity); (b) planning the action (which includes motivation and conceptualization); and (c) execution (which includes self-correction and verbal mediation). As a child moves in and out of a box, for example, she relies on imitation and experimentation of how to move her body in and out (ideation). Successful attempts also require initiation of movement and feedback from proprioceptors that allow the child to refine her ability to move in and out of the box.

Motor-planning problems are not caused by poor sensory processing but are the result of difficulties with the intermediary process of planning movement. That is, adequate motor planning requires a feedback system to give meaning to movement and a feed-forward system that allows the child to anticipate the next step – the strength or speed required to complete an activity, for example. All of this happens without the child ever consciously thinking about it. The ability to grade movement (select appropriate timing, force, speed) allows the child to vary the intensity of what he does. This enables the child to catch balls of different sizes, move on/off different playground equipment, and write with different-sized pencils, for example.

Special Difficulties for Children with Autism Spectrum Disorders

Typical motor-planning problems seen in children with autism spectrum disorders include postural dyspraxia (the inability to plan and imitate body postures), sequencing dyspraxia (poorly timed movements and poor bilateral coordination), oral and verbal dyspraxia (inability to demonstrate or imitate oral movements on verbal command), constructional dyspraxia (inability to assemble three-dimensional structures), and graphic dyspraxia (inability to plan and execute drawings) (DeGangi, 200; Trott et al., 1993).

Activation and Function of the Sensory Systems

SYSTEM	ACTIVATION	FUNCTION
Tactile (touch)	Contact with the skin	Enables us to explore environment (discriminative) and protect (protective)
Vestibular (balance)	Head movement, inner ear	Registers movement, helps us resist the pull of gravity
Proprioception (deep pressure to joints)	Stimulated by *active* movement through stretching and bending of joints and muscles	Sends information about movement, muscle tension, pressure, and muscles and space to central nervous system to support motor skill acquisition
Auditory (hearing)	Responds to movement, sound, and vibration	Enables us to receive, identify, discriminate, understand, respond to sound
Visual (sight)	Stimulated by light hitting retina	Provides information about physical properties and spatial relationships
Olfactory and Gustatory (smell and taste)	Nasal passages and tongue receptors	Provides information about properties of food and other environmental stimuli

SENSORY-PROCESSING MOTOR DEFICITS
Possible Causes and Play Supports

The following chart describes behaviors that are consistent with sensory-processing difficulties (distractibility, perseveration, impulsivity, awkward/clumsy) and provides simple classroom and play considerations to address these difficulties.

OBSERVABLE BEHAVIORS	PLAY SUPPORTS
Distractibility • Child may not be able to inhibit sensory input from visual, auditory, tactile stimuli • Child may be overly aware of environment (noise from a fan, slight movements of others in room, etc.)	• Use clearly organized materials • Keep area uncluttered • Control noise level and visual distractions • Incorporate toys/fidgets (mood changers) • Be aware of proximity of peers • Use scents to achieve and sustain attention
Perseveration • Child may have a limited play repertoire or poor ability to generalize across situations • Child may not know when to stop a behavior • Child may prefer repetitive activities for self-calming	• Determine sensory effects by carefully observing play choices • Find a motivating theme • Use physical prompts or cue cards to transition • Increase degree of difficulty at child's pace • Use familiar materials
Impulsivity • Child may be in high or low state of arousal due to too much or too little sensory input • Child may have poor motor planning and initiate or execute movement without adequate planning • Child may have a high pain threshold	• Use clear boundaries and visual cues • Stick to consistent structure • Motor child through the task • Minimize choices • Break down the task or game
Awkward/Clumsy • Child may have poor body awareness due to poor proprioceptive or vestibular processing, difficulties with eye-hand coordination, or lack of motor coordination • Child may have poor visual acuity • Child may have poor auditory processing (decreased listening skills) • Child may have low muscle tone resulting in poor endurance	• Provide sensory-motor program that focuses on body awareness and motor planning • Teach specific playground skills for peer play • Provide playground themes that are appropriate for age and development • Use obstacle courses and unfamiliar activities to teach problem solving • Use physical prompts or cue cards to help with motor planning • Use peer players to provide good role models for play

ENVIRONMENTAL FACTORS AND PLAY

The following suggestions outline factors to consider when setting up a play group in the classroom, clinic or home.

Optimal Times

- Children with neurological problems (e.g., inattention and distractibility issues and poor endurance) tend to tire easily and get disorganized. Keep activities brief for these children. Observe a child at play at different times during the day and adapt the schedule to best meet the child's needs.

- Precede fine-motor games or activities with gross-motor activities that include proprioception. For example, deep pressure to the muscles and joints in activities like wheelbarrow walking gives a child's nervous system input for organization before seated work games that require focused attention.

Age and Development

- The activities in this book are targeted for children 4 years through 12 years old. However, as always, the needs of individual children, regardless of age, must be considered when selecting an activity.

Organization

- Use boundaries such as carpet squares, taped boundaries, place mats, furniture, etc., to maintain play activities in a specified area. Boundaries help a child know where to stand and also help with body-spatial awareness.

- Make all play materials related to a specific theme readily available; cover up or remove toys that are not to be used during a given session to avoid distractions.

- Have ample supplies of clean-up materials on hand (e.g., towels, napkins).

Safety

- Think safety during all play activities (e.g., remove hanging equipment when not in use, replace caps on bubble containers, place mats on floor to avoid skidding).

- Use caution when adding scents to activities to affect arousal states. Children with allergies may be prohibited from working with specific scents.

- For children who are allergic, try using hypoallergenic materials (e.g., shaving cream and chalk).

NOTE: For anyone suffering from disease, illness, or injury, a physician should be consulted prior to play group participation.

Environmental Factors Schematic

By providing sensory integration strategies prior to Integrated Play Groups, children with atypical nervous systems such as many children with autism spectrum disorders (ASD) are able to participate more appropriately in peer play.

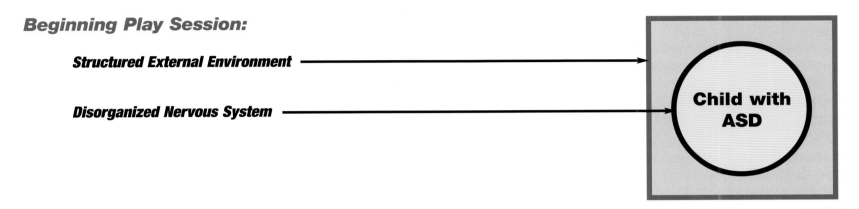

As the novice player's system begins to organize, the structure of the play group is modified.

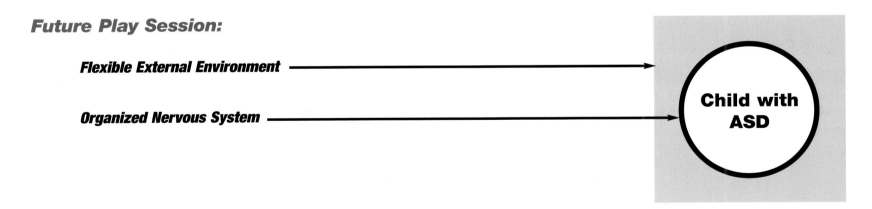

A child with autism spectrum disorders demonstrates a fragile, overly sensitive, disorganized nervous system that requires concrete structures or boundaries in order for the child to participate in peer play. These boundaries can be as simple as a hula hoop or carpet square to define a space. As the child's nervous system becomes more tolerant of environmental factors such as peers in close proximity during play, there is less need for structuring the environment so carefully (physical boundaries).

Play Materials Resource List

To be prepared to conduct the activities that follow, we recommend that you have the following materials on hand. If you are unable to locate them in local stores, they may be purchased from the companies listed under Resources below. In addition, we recommend that you stock a wide range of supplies (consumables).

Materials

Balance beam
Balance board
Bean bag chair
Bungee cords
Candy bubbles
Cooperband
Echo microphone
Environmental sound machine
  (nature sounds)

Glider swing
Gooey snakes and worms
Hammock swing
Hanging inner tube
Hoppity hop
Lycra/spandex
Parachute
Peanut ball
Platform swing

Pop-up squares/tunnels
Rapper snappers
Scented bubbles
Scooterboards
Stacking cones
t-stool
Variety of whistles
Wiggle cushion

Resources

Southpaw 1-800-228-1698   www.southpaw.com
Sportime 1-800-850-8602   www.abilitations.com
Therapy Shoppe 1-800-261-5590   www.therapyshoppe.com
Flaghouse 1-800-793-7900   www.flaghouse.com

Note. Guidelines for suspending equipment are available through Southpaw's suspension kit.

ASSESSMENT TOOLS

It is difficult to assess children on the autism spectrum using structured assessment protocols or developmental tests. There is not sufficient evidence to suggest that these standardized tests can elicit the full cooperation of the child with severe developmental challenges or demonstrate critical functional developmental capacities and important processing abilities (e.g., visual-spatial, motor planning, sensory modulation). In order to bring out the child's highest level of functioning, it is important to use clinical evaluation consisting of observation, discussion, and clinical judgment. Assessment should be a dynamic, ongoing process involving a functional developmental profile of each child (Greenspan, 2000).

Listed below are several assessment tools that we have used successfully with children with autism spectrum disorders. Therapists can use these tools as part of a comprehensive sensorimotor evaluation. Results from testing can be used to plan appropriate sensory-based play activities.

Sensory History

Sensory Profile, Dunn (1999)
This standardized parent survey looks at all areas of sensory processing, both seeking and avoiding: vestibular, auditory, tactile, gustatory, olfactory and proprioceptive. Responses are given numerical value and are compared to those of typically developing children. Results are reported as either typical, possible difference, or definite difference.

Functional Skill Assessment

School Function Assessment (SFA), Coster, Deeney, Haltiwanger, & Haley (1998)
The primary use of the SFA is to determine the student's current ability to participate successfully and fully in the educational program and the functional strengths and limitations affecting the student's ability to meet school expectations. The SFA provides a comprehensive base of information about the student's current level of participation in his or her educational programs and activities expected of or provided to his or her peers.

Clinical Observations

The child is observed in a variety of positions and postures during which the following areas are noted: muscle tone, strength, range of motion, residual primitive reflexes, postural security, motor planning, isolated finger movement, speed and coordination of movement, right/left discrimination, balance, protective extension, sensory processing, awareness of positions and movements of the body, grasp patterns and in-hand manipulation/use of functional tools.

Play Observations

Profile of Individual Play Development, Wolfberg (2003)
This evaluative summary provides information on a child's prevailing cognitive/symbolic play, social play, communicative functions and means and play preferences at different points in time as a way to measure growth and change.

Play Preferences

Play Preference Inventory, Wolfberg (2003)

This inventory is designed to record the play preferences of both novice and expert players as a way to identify and match children's play interests. Play preferences include children's fascinations with and attractions to toys or props, interactions with toys or props, and choice of play activities, play themes, and playmates.

Sensorimotor Development

The form on pp. 21-22 can be used to document sensory modulation, gross- and fine-motor skill development, motor planning skills, and attention, engagement, and purposeful problem-solving abilities during peer play activities. The profile documents growth and change over time (dates of assessment are numbered 1, #2, #3 and take place every three months). Therapists, teachers or parents can use this form when observing integrated play sessions to document progress.

Problem-Solving Worksheet

The worksheet on p. 25 is designed to be used to document a child's strengths, areas of concern, goals and objectives and treatment plan. The sample on p. 26 illustrates the functional issue of the worksheet.

Profile of Individual Sensorimotor Development
(Page 1 of 2)

Name: _____

Dates

CHARACTERISTICS	Assessment (1)	Assessment (2)	Assessment (3)	DESCRIPTION OF SKILL
GROSS-MOTOR SKILLS				1.
Functional for Play				
Limited Skills				2.
Emerging Skills				3.
No Skills				
FINE-MOTOR SKILLS				1.
Functional for Play				
Limited Skills				2.
Emerging Skills				3.
No Skills				
MOTOR PLANNING				1.
Functional Motor Planning				
Mild to Moderate Motor Planning Dysfunction				2.
Severe Motor Planning Dysfunction				3.

Profile of Individual Sensorimotor Development

(Page 2 of 2)

Name: _____

Dates

CHARACTERISTICS	Assessment (1)	Assessment (2)	Assessment (3)	DESCRIPTION OF SKILL
SENSORY MODULATION				1.
Max. Self-Regulated >75%				2.
Mod. Self-Regulated 50-75%				
Min. Self-Regulated >25%				3.
No Self-Regulated <25%				
ATTENTION, ENGAGEMENT, PURPOSEFUL AND PROBLEM-SOLVING BEHAVIOR				1.
Functionally engaged during play, purposeful problem solving				2.
Partially engaged and purposeful with limited complex problem solving				
Partially engaged with only fleeting purposeful behavior				3.
No affective engagement and minimal attention during play				

Comments based on results of the Profile of Individual Sensorimotor Development:

Profile of Individual Sensorimotor Development Framework

Definitions Used on the Profile of Sensorimotor Development

Gross-Motor and Fine-Motor Skills

(The following definitions are used to document both gross- and fine-motor skills)

Functional for Play
The child demonstrates age-appropriate gross- and fine-motor skills in peer play activities.

Limited Skills
The child is able to participate in some activities with peers without assistance, but requires assistance or adaptation for new activities. Child demonstrates some skills in expected age range but most skills are lower than chronological age. The child may demonstrate immature movement patterns and motor acts, but is unable to coordinate sequencing and timing of more mature motor skill activities.

Emerging Skills
The child has some gross- or fine-motor skills (e.g., walks on tip toes, jumps, crawls), but is unable to perform any skills in the expected age range. The child's movement patterns are restrained, and the variety of motor skills is limited. Problems with postural control, strength, endurance, balance and coordination are evident.

No Skills
The child is unable to functionally initiate gross- or fine-motor skills necessary for participation in play activities with peers.

Motor Planning

(All motor planning skills are assessed within the context of play)

Functional Motor Planning
The child demonstrates the ability to participate in play activities and themes with peers. She is able to execute novel motor activities, sequences, or routines, and is able to safely and accurately access play equipment and materials.

Mild to Moderate Motor Planning Dysfunction
The child has limited ability to plan and perform goal-directed movement, skilled or novel motor tasks. The child may appear clumsy (e.g., falls frequently, bumps into things, slumped body posture), and initiation of new movement sequences or newly organized plans of behavior is difficult. The child may demonstrate a fear of trying new things, may become easily frustrated during play, and may be very controlling of activities.

Severe Motor Planning Dysfunction
The child is unable to participate in novel activities. He requires rigid routines and structure for all activities. The child may be disruptive or aggressive, particularly when there is no external structure to organize the child, or may be very passive, preferring the repetition of certain favorite activities and resisting new activities. The child is unable to participate in play with peers without maximal adult facilitation.

Sensory Modulation

Maximally Self-Regulated
The child is able to modulate sensory information with accuracy (demonstrates internal capacity to modulate levels of arousal in response to sensory stimulation and make sense of the play environment greater than 75% of the time). The child is able to initiate, maintain and cease physical acts, delay her own actions during play (turn taking), and comply with others and general social expectations. There is an uninterrupted flow of play, which includes problem solving and being engaged during play with peers.

Moderately Self-Regulated
The child demonstrates the ability to participate with peers in play and comply with others and general social expectations without adult intervention 50-75% of the play time. The child begins to demonstrate the ability to problem-solve with peers and interact in a goal-directed activity but requires adult facilitation. The child begins to move into an "ebb and flow" of play or use appropriate interactions during play.

Minimally Self-Regulated
The child has difficulty attaining, maintaining, and changing his arousal state during peer play. The child may demonstrate intense periods of frustration and quick mood swings, moving from intense happiness to being overwhelmed and having tantrums. Adult facilitation is required throughout the play session. The child is able to rejoin the peer play with adult facilitation 25-50% of the time.

No Self-Regulation Skills
The child is unable to modulate sensory information with accuracy and make sense of the play environment. The child may be easily overwhelmed by changes in visual, auditory, or vestibular input. Adult facilitation is required throughout the peer play session to assist the child with sensory modulation.

Attention, Engagement, Purposeful and Problem-Solving Behaviors

The child is evaluated on her ability to modulate sensory information and change arousal states during peer play in response to environmental changes. The child's sustained attention and engagement (the ability to direct and focus cognitive activity on specific stimuli) is a requirement for information processing, demonstration of mature motor acts, initiation of peer interactions, and demonstration of problem solving within the context of a group (Greenspan & Wieder, 1997).

Problem-Solving Worksheet

NAME _____ DATE_____

STRENGTHS:

AREAS OF CONCERN:

QUESTIONS:

GOALS AND OBJECTIVES:

TREATMENT PLAN:

Problem-Solving Worksheet
SAMPLE

NAME _____John_____ DATE _____5/26/04_____

STRENGTHS:
• Actively explores environment
• Enjoys music and rhythm activities
• Able to follow two-step directives
• Plays with peers as an onlooker (able to imitate)

AREAS OF CONCERN:
• Low neurological threshold and easily over-aroused (sensitive to tactile and auditory input)
• Limited fine- and gross-motor skills (requires assistance in ball skill games and all art activities)
• Fleeting attention (difficulty sustaining attention for more than 2 minutes at a time, runs around the room and touches everything in non-purposeful way)

QUESTIONS:
1. What sensory system can be used to captivate attention and "hold" attention?
2. Can John respond to peer directives during play?
3. Would a visual schedule (play choices picked by group) help him during peer play?

GOALS AND OBJECTIVES: SHORT-TERM (6 months)
John will demonstrate improved self-regulation and sensory processing in order to participate in peer play activities.
a. John will participate as an active player with peers during a problem-solving activity with minimal adult redirect or facilitation.
b. John will respond to a peer question without adult assistance to restate or clarify 80% of the time.
c. John will initiate a play choice and enlist peer to help set the activity up with minimal adult facilitation.
d. John will participate in a messy art activity without overloading, demonstrated by his ability to complete the activity.

TREATMENT PLAN:
• 1/2 hour of sensory integration incorporating proprioceptive and vestibular input to focus attention and calm and organize John's nervous system.
• Rhythm and music to reinforce multistep activities that require sustained attention.
• Peers to pick three activities prior to play and list them on the chalkboard.

ACTIVITIES

Play becomes a balanced partnership when sensory integration and Integrated Play Groups are combined

How to Use the Activity Sheets

Before turning to the 40 activities that follow, please familiarize yourself with the way the activities are presented to save time in the long run.

- The activities are meant to be suggestions to get you started.

- Activities are theme based and designed to be used for children ages 4 years to 12 years old.

- On each activity page the foundation systems that are being addressed are highlighted in red.

- Materials used in each play activity are highlighted in blue.

- A page accompanies each activity for making notes of revisions or additions to the activity for future use. The note pages can be used to individualize materials and supplies for a child's sensory-processing style, clarify strategies in the environmental set-up that were successful, and develop ways to expand on the theme (see examples below).

Modification/Expansion

Pick and choose among activities, and adapt and modify depending on the physical and sensory needs of the novice player. Some activities may not be appropriate for all children. Activities should be chosen based on a child's developmental age, sensory profile, and likes and dislikes.

An example of a *modification* to an activity might be as follows:

Wild, Wild West!
- Use chairs for the group to sit on (as horses) for a child with poor motor coordination who may not be able to sit on a hoppity hop independently. If this option is used, make sure to note it on the Notes page under Materials.

Paint the Town Red
- Use hypoallergenic shaving cream for an allergic child. Note this on the Notes page under Supplies.

An example of an *expansion* to an activity might be as follows:

Animal Hospital
- Change the location of the activity (go outside in the sand box) and add a "receptionist" with a cash register who will check in the animals prior to their appointments. Note this on the Notes page under Set-up.

Activities and Their Developmental Foundations

ACTIVITIES	DEVELOPMENTAL FOUNDATIONS							
	Page Number	Vestibular	Proprioception	Tactile	Olfactory	Auditory	Gustatory	Motor
Wild, Wild West!	33	X	X	X		X		X
Power Peanut Pop	35	X	X			X		X
Tool Time	37		X	X		X		X
Boppin' Boxing!	39		X	X		X		X
Bumper Car Races	41	X	X	X		X		X
Searchin' Submarine	43	X	X	X		X		X
Flying Trapeze!	45	X	X	X		X		X
Mountain Climbing	47	X	X	X		X		X
Animal Hospital	49		X	X	X	X		X
Surf's Up!	51	X	X	X		X		X
Let's Go Fishing!	53	X	X	X		X	X	X
Shaving Cream Mystery	55		X	X	X	X		X
The Wiggly Worm	57		X	X		X		X
Hoop Challenge	59		X					X
It's a Circus!	61	X	X	X	X	X	X	X
"Simon Says" in Cubes	63		X	X		X		X
Frog Drop	65	X	X	X	X	X	X	X
Paint the Town!	67			X	X			X
The Magic School Bus	69		X	X		X	X	X
Jungle Adventure	71	X	X	X				X

Activities and Their Developmental Foundations

ACTIVITIES	Page Number	Vestibular	Proprioception	Tactile	Olfactory	Auditory	Gustatory	Motor
				DEVELOPMENTAL FOUNDATIONS				
Let's Go Camping!	73	X	X	X		X	X	X
Dress-Up	75			X	X	X	X	X
The Secret Garden	77		X	X	X			X
Sandfastic!	79		X	X				X
Chalkboard Challenge	81		X	X		X		X
The Launching Pad	83	X	X	X		X		X
Car Wash	85		X	X	X	X		X
The Bird Nest	87	X	X	X	X	X	X	X
Blow Off Some Steam!	89	X	X	X	X	X	X	X
Space Jump	91	X	X			X		X
Bounce and Switch	93	X	X			X		X
Car Rally	95		X	X		X		X
Follow the Leader	97	X	X	X	X	X	X	X
Let's Play House!	99		X	X	X	X	X	X
Cooking Class	101		X	X	X	X		X
Human Cannonball	103	X	X			X		X
Don't Rock the Boat!	105	X	X	X		X	X	X
Dinosaur Island	107	X	X	X	X	X		X
Restaurant's Open!	109		X	X		X	X	X
Blast-Off!	111	X	X			X		X

NOTES

Materials:

Set-up:

Supplies:

Wild, Wild West!

MATERIALS:

- bolster swing
- gold-painted rocks or tan bark
- hats and vests
- hoppity hops
- large ball
- long rope
- platform swing
- pop-up squares or tunnel
- pompoms
- squirt bottles or guns
- variety of whistles

Facilitator prompts to initiate play theme:

"Let's dress up! Who are you? Who's the sheriff? Who is the shop owner?"

"Ride into town on your horses (hoppity hops). Hold on to the reins (long rope) and say "giddy up" to make your horse go!"

"Give your horse some hay (pompoms)."

"Does everyone have their water pistol (squirt bottles, squirt guns, etc.)?"

"Let's go for a hunt for gold nuggets (painted rocks)."

"Get in the mine shaft. Watch out for falling rocks (cloth tunnel or pop-up squares and therapy balls)!"

"Blow your whistle when you find the gold!"

"Get on the stage coach (platform swing) so we can get out of town!"

Vestibular   **Proprioception**   **Tactile**   Olfactory   **Auditory**   Gustatory   **Motor**

NOTES

Materials:

Set-up:

Supplies:

Power Peanut Pop

MATERIALS:

- bolster swing
- music
- target
- yellow peanut ball

Facilitator prompts to initiate play theme:

"Let's see if we can make the peanut ball **pop up in the air!**"

"Everyone will need to do a job. I need someone to stand on the swing and move their body to make the swing go. Someone else will sit on the swing and kick the ball when it is rolled at them. Another person will roll the ball at the swing."

"The ball roller can call out *'ready, set, go!'* and then he has to catch the ball when it is kicked!"

"How high can the peanut ball go?"

"Can you switch places when the music **stops?**"

"Can you kick the ball at the hanging target?"

"How else can we pop up the ball?"

Vestibular	Proprioception	Tactile	Olfactory	Auditory	Gustatory	Motor

NOTES

Materials:

Set-up:

Supplies:

Tool Time

MATERIALS:

- Legos
- plastic nails, screws, nuts and bolts
- plumbing connectors
- PVC plumbing pipe
- rapper snappers
- wooden blocks
- assorted play tools
- connecting blocks
- pop beads

Facilitator prompts to initiate play theme:

"The tool shop is open. What should we build today?"

"Everybody, help to make the _____ (house, bridge, skyscraper)."

"What could we do with the pipes, rapper snappers, Legos, pop beads?"

"Can you use your drill to fix the ends of the structure?"

"Someone, help us saw the wood to fit into the house."

"Be careful! I think this end needs more support!"

| Vestibular | **Proprioception** | **Tactile** | Olfactory | **Auditory** | Gustatory | **Motor** |

NOTES

Materials:

Set-up:

Supplies:

Boppin' Boxing!

MATERIALS:

- bubbles
- hammock swing
- inflatable boxing gloves
- large ball

Facilitator prompts to initiate play theme:

"Get ready to rumble! Everybody, put on your gloves for the boxing match."

"How many times can you hit the ball without getting knocked over?"

"Can you use your other hand to hit the ball?"

"Who will be the champion boxer?"

"How many hits will you take before the next boxer has a turn?"

"Who can box while standing on one foot?"

"Watch out for the bubbles! Can you hit them too?"

Vestibular   **Proprioception**   **Tactile**   Olfactory   **Auditory**   Gustatory   **Motor**

NOTES

Materials:

Set-up:

Supplies:

Bumper Car Races

MATERIALS:

- bungee cords
- cones
- hanging inner tubes
- large balls
- music

Facilitator prompts to initiate play theme:

"Jump on the tire and let's bump our cars (inner tube) together!"

"When you hear the music, get on the tire on your tummy or sitting and get ready to play!"

"When the music stops, fall down on the floor!"

"Can you pick up all the cones on the floor while you lie on your tummy?"

"Who can roll the ball in between the two tires to crash the bumper cars?"

"Don't fall off your car!"

Vestibular   **Proprioception**   **Tactile**   Olfactory   **Auditory**   Gustatory   **Motor**

NOTES

Materials:

Set-up:

Supplies:

Searchin' Submarine

MATERIALS:

- bolster swing
- bubbles
- stacking cones
- felt board and fish
- flashlights
- piece of spandex
- sound machine

Facilitator prompts to initiate play theme:

"Everybody, climb into the submarine (bolster swing and spandex) **and let's go on an adventure."**

"Turn on your light beams (flashlights) **and let's see what we can find."**

"Do you hear the water rushing (sound machine) **past the sub?"**

"How many of you can shine your light on the great, big, giant shark?"

"Hold on tight. Let's go fast!"

"How many fish **can you scoop up under the sub?"**

"Everybody, point your beams at the floating bubbles!**"**

Vestibular   Proprioception   Tactile   Olfactory   Auditory   Gustatory   Motor

NOTES

Materials:

Set-up:

Supplies:

Flying Trapeze!

MATERIALS:

- bean bag chair
- inner tube
- soft blocks

- spandex trapeze bar
- graph paper and pencils

Facilitator prompts to initiate play theme:

"Today we are going to design a flying trapeze game."

"Let's use the blocks, bean bag chair, and trapeze bar to make a game."

"Who wants to be the first to take the challenge?"

"How far can you swing out and drop?"

"Does it work better if you get a push from a friend?"

"Who had the _____(longest, highest, shortest) jump?"

"Let's cheer for each friend as we take turns."

"We can make a graph to show our scores!"

Vestibular   Proprioception   Tactile   Olfactory   Auditory   Gustatory   Motor

NOTES

Materials:

Set-up:

Supplies:

Mountain Climbing

MATERIALS:

- bean bags
- bean bag chair
- bucket
- flashlight
- ramp
- rope
- various textures to put onto the ramp

Facilitator prompts to initiate play theme:

"Hold on to the rope and climb up to the top of the mountain (ramp)!"

"What can you find at the top of the mountain?"

"Carry the bucket of supplies to the top to attach to the ladder (rope)."

"Do you need a flashlight to see the hidden rocks?"

"Can you use the trapeze to rappel off the mountain and drop into the sea (blue bean bag chair)?"

"Watch out for the avalanche (flying bean bags)!"

"Everyone, climb over the obstacles on the mountain. Don't fall off!"

| Vestibular | Proprioception | Tactile | Olfactory | Auditory | Gustatory | Motor |

NOTES

Materials:

Set-up:

Supplies:

Animal Hospital

MATERIALS:

- play doctor's kit
- plastic animals
- shaving cream
- small tubs of water
- towels

Facilitator prompts to initiate play theme:

"**The** jungle animals **have been loaded in the truck and brought to our hospital.**"

"**Get the** doctor's kit **and supplies and let's inspect the animals!**"

"**Do any of the animals need a bath, their teeth brushed, a shot, bandages?**"

"**What sounds are your animals making?**"

"**Take turns using the magic cream** (shaving cream) **on your animal.**"

Vestibular   **Proprioception   Tactile   Olfactory   Auditory**   Gustatory   **Motor**

NOTES

Materials:

Set-up:

Supplies:

Surf's Up!

MATERIALS:

- blanket
- bubbles
- glider swing
- hanging spandex
- sound machine
- surfing music

Facilitator prompts to initiate play theme:

"Everyone will get a turn to ride the waves today. Step onto the surfboard (glider swing) and get ready to roll!"

"Who can swing over the board?"

"How rough is the ocean?"

"Can you ride the waves all the way back to the shore?" (Two players hold up blanket to make the waves.)

"Whose turn is next?"

"Now it's raining (bubbles). Don't let the rain drops touch your body."

"Can you jump up and over the wave (blanket)?"

| Vestibular | Proprioception | Tactile | Olfactory | Auditory | Gustatory | Motor |

NOTES

Materials:

Set-up:

Supplies:

Let's Go Fishing!

MATERIALS:

- fish
- fishing net
- fishing poles
- gummy worms
- long blocks for oars
- platform swing
- rope
- sound machine

Facilitator prompts to initiate play theme:

"Let's get into the deep, blue ocean and go fishing!"

"Get on the row boat (swing) and let's row out to sea!"

"Do you feel the waves rolling and can you hear the ocean sounds?"

"Look out into the ocean and see if you can see a fish."

"Use your fishing poles to catch a fish."

"What color fish did you catch?"

"Drop your fish into the net that your friend is holding up for you!"

"Can you catch a worm and eat it?"

"What should we do with all the fish we caught?"

Vestibular **Proprioception** **Tactile** Olfactory **Auditory** **Gustatory** **Motor**

NOTES

Materials:

Set-up:

Supplies:

Shaving Cream Mystery

MATERIALS:

- large tub of water
- scented shaving cream
- small plastic animals
- towels

Facilitator prompts to initiate play theme:

"Today we are going on a mystery hunt for animals."

"All of the animals are hiding in the shaving cream."

"Let's take turns 'hunting' in the shaving cream and see what we can find."

"What kind of animal did you find?"

"Where does your animal live?"

"What sounds does your animal make?"

"When we find all the animals, let's wash them in our magic bath!"

"Use the towels to dry them and then we can put them together and see who lives on the farm, in the zoo, or in the ocean!"

Vestibular   **Proprioception**   **Tactile**   **Olfactory**   **Auditory**   Gustatory   **Motor**

NOTES

Materials:

Set-up:

Supplies:

The Wiggly Worm

MATERIALS:

- drum music
- flashlights
- large ball
- t-shirt tube

Facilitator prompts to initiate play theme:

"Today we are going to pretend that we are a long, wiggly worm."

"Let's follow each other into the worm's skin (tube or tunnel) and get ready to wiggle."

"Who can push the big ball through the worm without stopping?"

"Can you make the worm roll over?"

"Take a flashlight inside the worm and see if you can be a 'glow worm' while you crawl through."

"Who can crawl and make the worm move to the beat of the music?"

Vestibular   **Proprioception**   **Tactile**   Olfactory   **Auditory**   Gustatory   **Motor**

NOTES

Materials:

Set-up:

Supplies:

Hoop Challenge

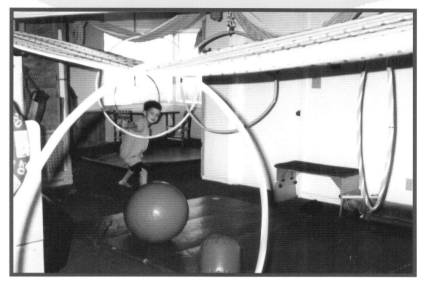

MATERIALS:

- assorted balls
- balloons
- hanging spandex
- hula hoops
- rope (20' long)

Facilitator prompts to initiate play theme:

"Everyone, take a turn and find a hula hoop **to hang from something in the room.**"

"**Let's see if we can throw** balloons **and** balls **through all the hoops!**"

"**Who can run through the course without getting knocked by a balloon?**"

"**Can you connect the hoops by making a** rope **go through all the hoops at the same time?**"

"**Let's go for the 'Groop Hoop Challenge.' Everyone, throw a ball or balloon through a hoop at the same time!**"

| Vestibular | **Proprioception** | Tactile | Olfactory | Auditory | Gustatory | **Motor** |

NOTES

Materials:

Set-up:

Supplies:

It's a Circus!

MATERIALS:

- ball
- balloons (blown up)
- bean bag chair
- bean bags
- costumes
- hula hoops
- large inner tube
- make-up
- parachute or spandex
- platform swing
- popcorn
- scented bubbles
- stool or soft blocks
- trapeze bar
- wigs & hats

Facilitator prompts to initiate play theme:

"Who wants to be a clown (make-up & costumes)**?"**

"All the clowns jump into the merry-go-round (platform swing with inner tube)**."**

"Get ready to punch the balloons **into the circus rings** (hula hoops)**."**

"Everyone line up to go on the flying trapeze (ball, spandex, and trapeze bar)**."**

"Can you fly into my circus cloud (trapeze bar **into** bean bag chair) **on the count of 3?"**

"Oh no, it's raining through the circus tent (scented bubbles **and players holding** parachute **or** spandex). **Catch the raindrops!"**

"Popcorn for sale; costs only one trick (somersault, hop, jump, etc.)."

Vestibular	Proprioception	Tactile	Olfactory	Auditory	Gustatory	Motor

NOTES

Materials:

Set-up:

Supplies:

"Simon Says" in Cubes

MATERIALS:

- music
- pop-up cubes

Facilitator prompts to initiate play theme:

"How many different ways can you make our cube move?"

"Let's play 'Simon Says' inside the cubes."

Simon Says:
- **jump up two times**
- **crawl out and in your cube**
- **switch cubes**
- **hook the cubes together and crawl through them**
- **hide under the cube**
- **move in the cube until the** music **stops**

Vestibular   **Proprioception   Tactile**   Olfactory   **Auditory**   Gustatory   **Motor**

NOTES

Materials:

Set-up:

Supplies:

Frog Drop

MATERIALS:

- bean bag frogs
- large mat
- popcorn
- targets
- trapeze bar
- whistles

Facilitator prompts to initiate play theme:

"The frogs have all hopped out of the pond."

"Let's find some lily pads (cardboard squares, soft blocks, small targets) and put them into the pond."

"Let's go on a hunt for the four missing frogs (heavy bean bag frogs)."

"When you find one, blow a whistle to tell your friends."

"Now you can hold onto the frog between your legs and swing over the pond on the trapeze and drop it onto a lily pad."

"After each of you has had a turn, we can figure out other ways to carry the frogs over the water."

"Can you catch the flies (popcorn) in our mouth like the frogs do?"

Vestibular   Proprioception   Tactile   Olfactory   Auditory   Gustatory   Motor

NOTES

Materials:

Set-up:

Supplies:

Paint the Town!

MATERIALS:

- cones for holding scented shaving cream
- food coloring
- glitter
- lots of towels

- shaving cream
- variety of paint brushes
- various flavorings (for smells)
- wooden blocks for buildings

Facilitator prompts to initiate play theme:

"Everybody, pick a paint can (cone and shaving cream) and a brush."

"Who wants blue? red? etc."

"Who can paint a road?"

"Do you need some buildings (blocks)?"

"Does anybody want a different color of paint?"

"Who wants glitter?"

"We have different smells (peppermint, lemon, etc.) for the paint; who wants some?"

"Time for clean-up."

"Take a dry towel to wipe up the paint."

| Vestibular | Proprioception | **Tactile** | **Olfactory** | Auditory | Gustatory | **Motor** |

NOTES

Materials:

Set-up:

Supplies:

The Magic School Bus

MATERIALS:

- balance beam
- cash register
- chairs for seats on the bus
- construction paper for making tickets
- hula hoops
- large inner tube
- obstacle course items
- plastic tubs
- popcorn and bowls
- pop-up school bus
- scissors for tickets
- soft blocks
- stuffed animals
- telephone (for emergency calls)
- trapeze bar

Facilitator prompts to initiate play theme:

"Let's take a ride in the magic school bus! Who wants to be the driver?"

"Where should the bus drive to first?"

"Does everyone have a ticket? When you get in, tell the driver where you want to go today."

"Join me in singing 'The Wheels on the Bus' while we drive down the street!"

"Let's stop at the popcorn stand and buy some popcorn."

"Let's stop at the pet store and find an animal to bring on our trip."

"Let's stop at the park and move through the obstacle course."

"Are we going on the bumpy road?" (move bus up and down)

Vestibular   Proprioception   Tactile   Olfactory   Auditory   Gustatory   Motor

NOTES

Materials:

Set-up:

Supplies:

Jungle Adventure

MATERIALS:

- balance beam
- bean bag chair
- gooey snakes and worms
- koosh balls
- large soft blocks
- long rope (20')
- rope ladder
- spandex
- target

Facilitator prompts to initiate play theme:

"We are traveling to the deep jungle. The monkeys are chasing us and we need to escape!"

"Climb up to the top of the tree (rope ladder)."

"Grab a hanging branch (spandex) and swing over the river (target)."

"Don't get stuck in the quicksand (bean bag chair)!"

"Watch out for the flying monkeys (koosh balls). Don't let them hit you!"

"Walk along the large snake (large rope) and across the rickety bridge (soft blocks) and down the narrow passage (balance beam) and then jump to safety!"

"Can you catch one of the falling snakes or worms (gooey snakes and worms thrown on the ceiling)?"

Vestibular   Proprioception   Tactile   Olfactory   Auditory   Gustatory   Motor

NOTES

Materials:

Set-up:

Supplies:

Let's Go Camping!

MATERIALS:

- animals (cardboard pictures; stuffed)
- flashlights
- hanging spandex
- Lite Brite board and pegs
- marshmallows
- pop-up tent or cube
- soft blocks
- sound machine
- stars
- sticks
- tissue paper, red and yellow
- whistles

Facilitator prompts to initiate play theme:

"We are going on a camp-out! Everyone, get a flashlight and a whistle in case we see any bears."

"Pop up the tent and climb inside. Can you hear the sounds of the forest?"

"Shine your lights on the stars (glow-in-the-dark stars) and on the animals (cardboard pictures or stuffed animals) hiding in the forest."

"I see a bear. Can you find him?"

"Let's build a campfire (use soft blocks and crushed-up tissue paper) and then roast marshmallows to eat!"

"Who can sing a campfire song?"

"Let's use the Lite Brite to make a pattern inside the tent."

"Climb inside the hammock (spandex) and shine your lights on the stars."

| Vestibular | Proprioception | Tactile | Olfactory | Auditory | Gustatory | Motor |

NOTES

Materials:

Set-up:

Supplies:

Dress-Up

MATERIALS:

- accessories
- camera (optional)
- dolls
- dress-up clothes
- full-length mirror
- lotion
- make-up
- music
- tea party supplies

Facilitator prompts to initiate play theme:

"**Who wants to help get the** dress-up clothes**?**"

"**Where does the** mirror **go?**"

"**Does anyone want this** (feather boa, hat, etc.)**?**"

"**Are you planning a parade in your fancy clothes?**"

"**Who wants their picture taken** (camera)**?**"

"**Does anyone need** lotion **or** make-up**?**"

"**Who wants to turn on the** music**?**"

"**Who needs help fastening their clothes?**"

"**Can you ask your friend to help?**"

"**Let's have a tea party** (cups, saucers, tea pot, cookies)**.**"

Vestibular	Proprioception	**Tactile**	**Olfactory**	**Auditory**	**Gustatory**	**Motor**

NOTES

Materials:

Set-up:

Supplies:

The Secret Garden

MATERIALS:

- baskets
- buckets with dirt
- crepe paper
- gloves filled with rice
- markers
- pipe cleaners
- pots
- scoops
- seeds
- squirt bottles
- tongue depressors
- watering cans or squirt bottles
- wheelbarrow

Facilitator prompts to initiate play theme:

"Let's plant a garden."

"Where do you want to plant your flowers?" (kids are walking along a path; some are pushing wheelbarrows, others are carrying heavy buckets with dirt).

"Pick up the flowers (gloves filled with rice) along the path and throw them into the gardening basket."

"Now you can choose your soil and what you want to plant (seeds)."

"Who knows what you need for digging?"

"Let's fill your watering cans and sprinkle water on our garden."

"Let's make plant stakes (tongue depressors and markers) so you'll know what is going to grow."

"We can make some flowers (crepe paper and pipe cleaners)."

Vestibular   **Proprioception**   **Tactile**   **Olfactory**   Auditory   Gustatory   **Motor**

NOTES

Materials:

Set-up:

Supplies:

Sandfastic!

MATERIALS:

- buckets
- feathers, rocks, jewels, straws
- plastic animals
- rakes
- sand
- shovels
- towels
- water

Facilitator prompts to initiate play theme:

"Can we make a giant castle out of sand?"

"What should we dig with? What should we use to mold the sand?"

"Who can fill up water buckets and carry them over to our area?"

"Mix the sand and water in your buckets. Now, what will happen when it is turned over?"

"Let's dig a moat around the castle. Pour the water in and see if it works."

"What animals can hide in the moat?"

"We can use the feathers, rocks, jewels, and straws to decorate the castle."

Vestibular	**Proprioception**	**Tactile**	Olfactory	Auditory	Gustatory	**Motor**

NOTES

Materials:

Set-up:

Supplies:

Chalkboard Challenge

MATERIALS:

- chalk
- chalkboard
- large balls
- squirt bottles
- towels

Facilitator prompts to initiate play theme:

"Today, we will have the great 'chalkboard challenge'."

"Each of you can get a ball to sit on."

"One person will be in charge of the chalk. You will need to ask your friend to 'pass the chalk' when you are ready to draw."

"What are you making?"

"Let's describe our drawings to our friends."

"Can you all make a drawing together?"

"Use the squirt bottles to wash away your drawing. Wipe the board clean with the towels."

| Vestibular | **Proprioception** | **Tactile** | Olfactory | **Auditory** | Gustatory | **Motor** |

NOTES

Materials:

Set-up:

Supplies:

The Launching Pad

MATERIALS:

- assorted balls
- beach ball
- bean bags
- bubbles
- bucket
- koosh ball
- large piece of spandex
- music
- target
- t-stools

Facilitator prompts to initiate play theme:

"This is **MISSION IMPOSSIBLE**: Your job is to launch as many things as possible off your launching pad today without any member of the team falling off the t-stool."

"Everyone, sit on a t-stool in a circle and hold onto the launching pad (piece of spandex)."

"Decide who the leader will be – the one who makes the (ready, set, go) calls."

"Can you bounce the koosh balls off the pad into the bucket?"

"Can you launch the ball in the air 10 times in a row?"

"What will happen if we try to launch the bean bags?"

"Do you think we can launch the beach ball to the beat of the music?"

Vestibular   **Proprioception**   **Tactile**   Olfactory   **Auditory**   Gustatory   **Motor**

NOTES

Materials:

Set-up:

Supplies:

Car Wash

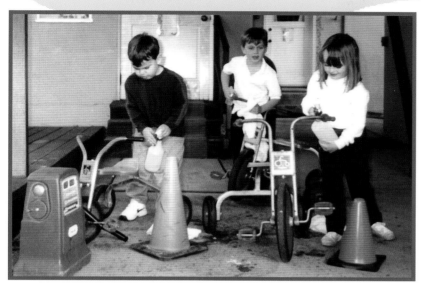

MATERIALS:

- cones
- liquid soap (baby shampoo)
- rags or towels
- rapper snappers
- scooter boards (2)
- shaving cream
- squirt bottles
- trikes, bikes, etc.
- water

Facilitator prompts to initiate play theme:

"**Everybody carry car wash supplies** (squirt bottles, rags, shaving cream)**.**"

"**Who wants to help fill the squirt bottles?**"

"**Who wants to be the squirter?**"

"**Can all of you wash at the same time?**"

"**Show us how a car washing machine works**" (two kids **sitting on** scooter boards **hold both hands, making the washing machine go**).

"**Do you need to fill up your car** (trike) **with gas** (rapper snapper tubes)**?**"

"**Time to wash and dry the cars.**"

Vestibular	**Proprioception**	**Tactile**	**Olfactory**	**Auditory**	Gustatory	**Motor**

NOTES

Materials:

Set-up:

Supplies:

The Bird Nest

MATERIALS:

- balls
- bean bags
- candy bubbles
- feathers
- gummy worms
- hanging spandex
- heavy bean bags
- pillows
- sound machine

Facilitator prompts to initiate play theme:

"Let's pretend we are baby birds and let's build a bird nest (hanging spandex)."

"What kinds of things do you want in your nest?" (bean bags, pillows, balls)

"Can you hear the other birds in the forest (sound machine)?"

"Who can catch a hanging worm (gummy worm) with their mouth?"

"Here comes the mommy bird who will feed you. Open your mouths to catch your food (candy bubbles)."

"Can you make your nest sway, bounce, open, or close?"

"All birds can fly around the room and choose another nest to visit."

"Let's blow feathers from one nest to another."

Vestibular	Proprioception	Tactile	Olfactory	Auditory	Gustatory	Motor

NOTES

Materials:

Set-up:

Supplies:

Blow off Some Steam!

MATERIALS:

- blow darts
- blow pens
- bubble wands
- candy bubbles
- peppermint oil

- popcorn
- target
- tire swing or rocking boat
- whistles

Facilitator prompts to initiate play theme:

"Today we can use our mouths to blow off steam!"

"Let's get into the steamboat (rocking boat or tire swing). Use your whistles to give us power to move the boat!"

"Here come the invaders (large hanging target)! Grab your blow gun (blow darts) and shoot them away!"

"When the boat is really working, the peppermint bubbles fly out of the engine!"

"How fast can you go? Can you catch a bubble in your mouth?"

"The boat needs a sign. Let's use the blow pen to make a sign with the name of our boat on it."

"Let's eat some popcorn to give us more energy!"

Vestibular	Proprioception	Tactile	Olfactory	Auditory	Gustatory	Motor

NOTES

Materials:

Set-up:

Supplies:

Space Jump

MATERIALS:

- hanging spandex
- hula hoops
- large ball
- large inner tube
- small balls
- space music
- tire swing

Facilitator prompts to initiate play theme:

"Today we are going to be astronauts and fly around in outer space!"

"Everyone, get in the tire swing and let's do the count-down to blast-off!"

"Get in your space suit (a piece of hanging spandex) and jump over the meteors (balls rolling on the floor)."

"Hold on tight to your spacesuit and see if you can jump on top of Saturn (large ball in inner tube)!"

"When I say '1, 2, 3, SWITCH!,' move to another space suit."

"Can anyone climb from one space suit to another without touching the floor? (move from hanging spandex to spandex)."

"Use your space suit to jump into the hoop!"

Vestibular   **Proprioception**   Tactile   Olfactory   **Auditory**   Gustatory   **Motor**

NOTES

Materials:

Set-up:

Supplies:

Bounce and Switch

MATERIALS:

- balance board
- hoppity hop
- hula hoop
- large ball
- swing

- tire
- trampoline
- trapeze bar
- t-stool

Facilitator prompts to initiate play theme:

"**Each of you pick a piece of equipment to sit on, swing on, jump on, or bounce on** (trampoline, ball in tire, swing)**.**"

"**Let's put ourselves in a circle with our equipment.**"

"**Everyone can count to 10. While you count, you bounce, swing or jump on your equipment.**"

"**When we say '10' it is time to switch positions!**"

"**Everybody ready? Here we go!**"

"**This time let's sing a song and then switch!**"

Vestibular   Proprioception   Tactile   Olfactory   Auditory   Gustatory   Motor

NOTES

Materials:

Set-up:

Supplies:

Car Rally

MATERIALS:

- assorted small cars
- blocks
- construction paper
- foam wedge
- heavy cardboard
- long board for ramp
- markers
- plastic tubes
- slinky
- stopwatch
- whistle

Facilitator prompts to initiate play theme:

"Let's get ready to rumble! Everyone pick a car for the car rally."

"We need to design a tough course for the cars."

"We can use a ramp (long board) and design tunnels for the cars to go through (blocks, tubes, cardboard)."

"How could we use the slinky?"

"Can someone make a jump (foam wedge, blocks, cardboard) for the cars?"

"Line up the cars at the top. Someone, get the stopwatch and be the time keeper. Who will blow the whistle to start the cars?"

"Let's design a score sheet. Name your car and we will time each race!"

Vestibular	**Proprioception**	**Tactile**	Olfactory	**Auditory**	Gustatory	**Motor**

NOTES

Materials:

Set-up:

Supplies:

Follow the Leader

MATERIALS:

- balance beam
- balls
- bean bags and target
- hula hoops
- large wooden blocks

- scented bubbles
- stomp-and-catch board
- straws and cotton balls
- tire swing
- trapeze bar

Facilitator prompts to initiate play theme:

"Each of you will get a turn to be the leader through a three-step obstacle course."

"Choose three activities that you like to play and demonstrate them for the group."

"The leader can help the followers by holding their hand, saying instructions, or by demonstrating."

"After everybody has had a turn, let's all pick one activity to add to a big obstacle course."

"Let's design the course to use activities for our muscles, eyes, ears, and mouths."

Vestibular   Proprioception   Tactile   Olfactory   Auditory   Gustatory   Motor

NOTES

Materials:

Set-up:

Supplies:

Let's Play House!

MATERIALS:

- bean bag chair
- broom
- child-size kitchen furniture
- dolls and doll clothes
- dust pan
- large cardboard box
- play food
- pots and pans
- scented dish soap
- shopping cart
- snack (goldfish, popcorn, etc.)
- stuffed animals
- tub of water & towels
- water or juice

Facilitator prompts to initiate play theme:

"Who wants to help get out the food?"

"Where should we put the table, stove, etc.?"

"Who is the mommy, daddy, baby, etc.?"

"What does the baby need to drink?"

"What do you want for a snack?"

"What should the box be?"

"What do you need to wash the dishes?"

"Does the baby need a bath?"

"Who wants to feed the animals a carrot, hamburger, cookie, etc.?"

"Where does the bean bag go?"

Vestibular   **Proprioception   Tactile   Olfactory   Auditory   Gustatory   Motor**

NOTES

Materials:

Set-up:

Supplies:

Cooking Class

MATERIALS:

- aprons
- assorted scents
- chef hats
- cookie cutters
- cooking utensils
- cups, bowls
- garlic press
- glitter
- marbles
- microphone
- play dough
- rolling pin
- scissors

Facilitator prompts to initiate play theme:

"Today we are going to pretend that we are on a TV cooking show."

"Each of you can choose special ingredients (play dough, glitter, marbles, scents, etc.) for your favorite recipe."

"We can use the cooking utensils and tools (rolling pin, cookie cutters, garlic press, scissors) to make our treats."

"When you are finished preparing your dish, you can present it to the group."

"Who wants to use the microphone for their presentation?"

"Bon appetit!"

Vestibular	Proprioception	Tactile	Olfactory	Auditory	Gustatory	Motor

NOTES

Materials:

Set-up:

Supplies:

Human Cannonball

MATERIALS:

- ceiling hooks
- floor mats
- large therapy ball
- medicine ball
- soft blocks or pylons
- spandex

Facilitator prompts to initiate play theme:

"Everybody, help stack the blocks for our human cannonball to knock over."

"Who wants to be the cannonball first?"

"Climb into the cannon (spandex hung from the ceiling) and let your friends give you a push to knock over the tower!"

"What other things could we use for a target?"

"Could we try to put this ball (medicine ball) into the cannon and knock over another tower?

Vestibular   **Proprioception**   Tactile   Olfactory   **Auditory**   Gustatory   **Motor**

NOTES

Materials:

Set-up:

Supplies:

Don't Rock the Boat!

MATERIALS:

- beans, jewels, marbles
- fishing poles
- long blocks for oars
- markers and paper
- mats
- plastic bags and goldfish snacks
- rocking board
- rope
- soft blocks
- sound machine
- treasure chest

Facilitator prompts to initiate play theme:

"Let's build a boat to take out into the ocean."

"Can we use the soft blocks, rocking board, and mats to make a boat?"

"What other things do we need for our sea voyage (rope, oars, fishing poles)?"

"Can you hear the sounds of the ocean (sound machine)?"

"Look at the sunken treasure chest! Someone, swim out to get it!"

"What's inside (beans, jewels, marbles)?"

"Oh no, man overboard! Someone throw him a rope!"

"Can you catch anything to eat (bags of goldfish snacks)?"

"Let's use the markers and paper to make a map of our sea voyage!"

Vestibular	Proprioception	Tactile	Olfactory	Auditory	Gustatory	Motor

NOTES

Materials:

Set-up:

Supplies:

Dinosaur Island

MATERIALS:

- assorted dinosaurs
- balance boards, 3
- blow darts
- inner tube
- large ball
- peppermint shaving cream
- squirt bottles
- towels

Facilitator prompts to initiate play theme:

"Today we are going to have a dinosaur challenge."

"Everyone can get a balance board to stand on while we make an island (inner tube and ball) on the table."

"Can you pick out some of your favorite dinosaurs. Get them ready to climb to the top of the island!"

"Let's add some snow and ice (peppermint shaving cream) to the island to make the climb more daring!"

"How many dinosaurs can stay on top without falling off?"

"What happens when the rain starts?" (kids use squirt bottles to squirt dinosaurs)

"Now what happens to the dinosaurs when the arrows (blow darts) fly?"

Vestibular   **Proprioception**   **Tactile**   **Olfactory**   **Auditory**   Gustatory   **Motor**

NOTES

Materials:

Set-up:

Supplies:

Restaurant's Open!

MATERIALS:

- cash register
- chef's hat
- menus
- notepad and pencil
- plastic dishes
- plastic food
- play dough
- play money
- rolling pin and cookie cutters
- snacks (m&m's, goldfish, popcorn, etc.)
- storefront
- table and chairs
- telephone
- towels
- tubs for washing dishes

Facilitator prompts to initiate play theme:

"Everybody, pick a job (cash register, waiter, cook, dishwasher, etc.) for the restaurant."

"What are the specials today?"

"What can I buy for one dollar?"

"Do you take phone orders?"

"Waitress, can you write down my order?"

"This is delicious apple pie. May I have some more?"

"Is the chef able to bake me a batch of cookies to take home?"

Vestibular   **Proprioception**   **Tactile**   Olfactory   **Auditory**   **Gustatory**   **Motor**

NOTES

Materials:

Set-up:

Supplies:

Blast-Off!

MATERIALS:

- bean bags
- flashlights
- glow-in-the-dark stars
- inner tube
- koosh balls
- planet stickers
- platform swing
- sound machine
- sweatshirt tube

Facilitator prompts to initiate play theme:

"**Everybody, jump in the spaceship** (platform swing) **and let's go to** _____ **(Mars)!**"

"**Let's shoot** (koosh balls) **at the flying aliens!**"

"**Watch out for flying meteors** (bean bags)**!**"

"**Use your laser beams** (flashlights) **to find the next planet we will travel to!**"

"**Can you hear the sound of the ... (spaceship, universe, aliens, etc.)** (sound machine)**?**"

"**Crawl through the magic tube** (sweatshirt tube) **and land on the planet of** _____ **(Mars)!**"

Vestibular   **Proprioception**   Tactile   Olfactory   **Auditory**   Gustatory   **Motor**

Appendix A

THE DEVELOPMENTAL PATHWAYS FOR KIDS MODEL
Combining Sensory Integration and Integrated Play Groups

Common terms in the literature when defining play include *intrinsic motivation, joy* or *enjoyment*. According to Piaget (1962), primitive play begins with a set of sensory-motor behaviors. Play is the strategy that children use to develop sensory, motor, cognitive, communication, and social competence. Development in one domain directly affects development in another, called secondary circular reactions (Piaget, 1962). Ayres (1979) believed that sensory integration occurred primarily in early play experiences. Describing sensory integration developmentally, she noted that the child organizes behavior through successful adaptive responses to sensation. For example, with successful outcomes (*play is fun*), the child is motivated to try more complex and challenging tasks, leading to an upward spiraling of development. In addition, play provides the foundation for later roles such as student, friend, and so forth (Royeen, 1997).

According to Wolfberg and colleagues (2001), "Enhancing the peer relations and play of children with autistic spectrum disorder constitute major challenges for parents, educators and therapists" (p. 61). A frame of reference that emphasizes play as a means as well as an outcome includes the sensory integration approach.

As school-based occupational and physical therapy moves more and more into the full inclusion model, it is time to revisit play as a tool for intervention. Therapists as well as parents, teachers, and others play a valuable role when they enhance the play and social experiences of children with special needs on the playground (Nabors & Badawi, 1997). Due to their prominent characteristics, without appropriate intervention, children with autism spectrum disorders are likely to remain isolated from their peer group and lead impoverished play lives (Wing & Gould, 1979). One of the best ways for young children with special needs to practice using newly acquired skills is in a play format. The use of child-initiated learning experiences capitalizes on the child's attention and motivation. Play is the accepted learning mode for nearly all children, including those with special needs (Widerstrom, 1995).

At Developmental Pathways for Kids, we have successfully combined physical therapy, occupational therapy, and speech and language therapy with Integrated Play Groups (see p. 115) during regularly scheduled therapy sessions. Our treatment approach utilizes a variety of methods of sensory stimulation (vestibular, tactile, proprioceptive, visual, auditory, gustatory, and olfactory) and provides building blocks for functional skills. The therapist designs a play session to incorporate sensory strategies that will support the self-regulation and sensory modulation of each novice player. A supportive, structured external environment allows the novice to begin to organize internally and move to an optimal learning state. Skills are not taught but are allowed to emerge spontaneously as foundations develop; therefore, play is the adaptive response to the *just-right challenge*. Play becomes a balanced partnership when sensory integration and Integrated Play Groups are the supporting foundation!

For more information contact us at: www.developmentalpathways.com,
452 Grand Street, Redwood City, CA 94062 (650) 366-0486

Appendix B

INTEGRATED PLAY GROUPS (IPG) MODEL
Guiding Children on the Autism Spectrum in Peer Relations and Play

FACT SHEET ON INTEGRATED PLAY GROUPS (IPG) MODEL

What Are Integrated Play Groups?

The Integrated Play Groups model was created by Pamela Wolfberg, Ph.D. (author, educator, and researcher), to address the unique and complex challenges children on the autism spectrum experience in peer relations and play. Integrated Play Groups consist of small groups of children on the autism spectrum (novice players) and typical peers/siblings (expert players), who regularly play together under the guidance of a qualified adult facilitator (play guide).

What Is the Purpose of Integrated Play Groups?

Research shows that peer play experiences are a vital part of children's learning, development, and culture. Children on the autism spectrum face many obstacles playing and socializing with peers. Integrated Play Groups are designed to enhance children's social interaction, communication, play, and imagination. An equally important focus is on teaching the peer group to be more accepting, responsive, and inclusive of children who relate and play in different ways.

Who May Participate in Integrated Play Groups?

Integrated Play Groups are customized as part of a child's individual education/therapy program. The model is appropriate for pre-school/elementary-aged children (3 to 11 years old). Play groups are made up of 3-5 children, with a higher ratio of expert than novice players. Novice players include children of all abilities on the autism spectrum and children with related special needs. Expert players include typical peers/siblings with strong social, communication, and play skills.

Where and When Do Integrated Play Groups Take Place?

Integrated Play Groups take place in natural play environments within school, home, therapy, or community settings. Play groups generally meet twice a week for 30- to 60-minute sessions over a 6- to 12-month period. Sessions are carried out in specially designed play spaces that include a wide range of motivating materials and activities.

How Does an Integrated Play Group Work?

Play sessions are tailored to the children's unique interests, abilities, and needs. The adult methodically guides novice and expert players to engage in mutually enjoyed play activities that encourage reciprocal social interaction, communication, and imagination such as pretending, constructing, art, music, movement, and interactive games. Gradually, the children learn how to play together with less and less adult support.

What Are the Benefits of Integrated Play Groups?

As demonstrated through award-winning research, novice players have benefited in the areas of social interaction, communication, language, representational play and related symbolic activity (writing and drawing). Expert players have benefited by showing greater self-esteem, awareness, empathy, and acceptance of individual differences. Both novice and expert players have formed mutual friendships while having fun together.

Pamela J. Wolfberg, Ph.D., is assistant professor at San Francisco State University and co-founder of the Autism Institute on Peer Relations and Play. As creator of the Integrated Play Groups model, she leads efforts to develop inclusive peer play programs for children within the United States, Canada, Europe, and Asia. Dr. Wolfberg is the recipient of several distinguished awards for scholarship and research. She is widely published and the author of *Play and Imagination in Children with Autism* (New York: Teachers College Press, 1999), and *Peer Play and the Autism Spectrum: The Art of Guiding Children's Socialization and Imagination* (Shawnee Mission, KS: Autism Asperger Publishing Company, 2003).

For more information, contact:

Autism Institute on Peer Relations and Play – Center for Integrated Play Groups
web site: www.autisminstitute.com or www.wolfberg.com
E-mail: playgroups@wolfberg.com
415/753-5669

Pamela J. Wolfberg, Ph.D.
Assistant Professor
Dept. of Special Education
San Francisco State University
1600 Holloway Ave
San Francisco, CA 94132

REFERENCES AND SUGGESTED READINGS

Ayres, A. J. (1979). *Sensory integration and the child*. Los Angeles: Western Psychological Services.

Ayres, A. J. (1982). *Developmental dyspraxia and adult onset apraxia.* Torrance, CA: Sensory Integration International.

Ayres, A. J., & Tickle, L. S. (1980). Hyper-responsivity to touch and vestibular procedures by autistic children. *American Journal of Occupational Therapy*, 34, 375-381.

Baraneck, G. T., Foster, L. G., & Berkson, G. (1997). Tactile defensiveness and stereotypical behaviors. *American Journal of Occupational Therapy*, *51*(2), 91-95.

Berry, R., & Fuge, G. (2000). *Developmental pathways for kids: Individual profile of sensory motor development.* Redwood City, CA: Authors.

Bundy, A. C. (2002). Play theory and sensory integration. In A. G. Fisher, E. A. Murray, & A. C. Bundy (Eds.), *Sensory integration: Theory and practice* (2nd ed., pp. 48-67). Philadelphia, PA: F. A. Davis.

Coling, M. C., & Garret, J. N. (1995). *Activity-based intervention guide*. Tucson, AZ: Therapy Skill Builders.

Coster, W., Deeney, T., Haltiwanger, J., & Haley, S. (1998). *School Function Assessment*. San Antonio, TX: Therapy Skill Builders.

DeGangi, G. A. (2000). *Pediatric disorders of regulation in affect and behaviors.* San Diego: Academic Press.

DeGangi, G. A., & Greenspan, S. I. (1988). The development of sensory functions in infants. *Physical and Occupational Therapy in Pediatrics*, *8*(3), 21-33.

Dunn, W. (1991). The sensorimotor systems: A framework for assessment and intervention. In F. P. Orelove & S. D. Sobsey (Eds.), *Educating children with multiple disabilities: A transdisciplinary approach* (pp. 33-78). Baltimore: Paul H. Brookes.

Dunn, W. (1999). *Sensory Profile*. San Antonio, TX: The Psychological Corporation.

Dunn, W., Brown, C., & McGuigan, A. (1994). The ecology of human performance: A framework considering the effect of context. In R. P. Cotrell (Ed.), *Perspectives on purposeful activity: Foundations & future of occupational therapy* (pp. 131-144). Bethesda, MD: American Occupational Therapy Association.

Fisher A. G. (1991). Vestibular-proprioceptive processing and bilateral integration and sequencing deficits. In A. G. Fisher, E. A. Murray, & A. C. Bundy (Eds.), *Sensory integration: Theory and practice* (pp. 71-107). Philadelphia, PA: F. A. Davis.

Fisher A. G., & Dunn, W. (1983). Tactile defensiveness: Historical perspectives, new research. A theory grows. *Sensory Integration Special Interest Section Newsletter, 6*(2), 1-2.

Greenspan, S. I. (2000). *Clinical practice guidelines: Redefining the standards of care for infants, children, and families with special needs.* Bethesda, MD: Interdisciplinary Council on Developmental and Learning Disorders.

Greenspan, S. I., & Wieder, S. (1997). Developmental patterns and outcomes in infants and children with disorders relating and communicating: A chart review of 200 cases of children with autistic spectrum diagnoses. *Journal of Developmental and Learning Disorders, 1*, 87-141.

Greenspan, S. I., & Wieder, S. (1998). *The child with special needs*. Reading, MA: Merloyd Laurence.

Greenspan, S. I., & Wieder, S. (1999). A functional developmental approach to autism spectrum disorders. *Journal of the Association for Persons with Severe Handicaps* (JASH), *24*(3), 147-161.

Haron, M., & Henderson, A. (1985). Active and passive touch in developmentally dyspraxic and normal boys. *Journal of Research in Occupational Therapy, 5*, 102-112.

Higley, A.C., & Leatham, P. (1998). *Aromatherapy A to Z*. Carlsbad, CA: Hay House Inc.

Kranowitz, C. S. (1998). *The out of sync child*. New York: Skylight Press Book, The Berkely Publishing Group.

Mailloux, Z. (1992). Explore the sense of touch. *Sensory Integration Quarterly, 20*(2), 10-11.

Myles, B. S., Cook, K. T., Miller, N., Rinner, L., & Robbins, L. A. (2000). *Asperger Syndrome and sensory issues: Practical solutions for making sense of the world*. Shawnee Mission, KS: Autism Asperger Publishing Company.

Nabors, L., & Badawi, M. (1997). Playground interactions for preschool-age children with special needs. *Physical & Occupational Therapy in pediatrics in Pediatrics, 17*(3), 21-25.

Piaget, J. (1962). *Play, dreams and imitation in childhood*. New York: W. W. Norton & Company.

Reisman, J. E., & King, L. J. (1993). *Making contact: Sensory integration and autism*. Peoria, IL: Division of Media/Learning Systems Continuing Education Programs of America.

Royeen, C. B. (1997). Play as occupation and as an indicator of health. In B. E. Chandler (Ed.), *The essence of play: A child's occupation* (pp. 1-12). Bethesda, MD: The American Occupational Therapy Association.

Siegel, B. (2003). *Helping children with autism learn*. New York: Oxford University Press.

Trott, M. C., Laurel, M., & Windeck, S. L. (1993). *Sensibilities: Understanding sensory integration*. Tucson, AZ: Therapy Skill Builders.

Widerstrom, A. H. (1995). *Achieving learning goals through play*. Tucson, AZ: Therapy Skill Builders.

Wing, L., & Gould, J. (1979). Severe impairments of social interaction and associated abnormalities in children: Edipemiology and classification. *Journal of Autism and Developmental Disorders*, *9*, 11-29.

Wolfberg, P. J. (1999). *Play and imagination in children with autism*. New York: Teachers College Press.

Wolfberg, P. J. (2003). *Peer play and the autism spectrum: The art of guiding children's socialization and imagination*. Shawnee Mission, KS: Autism Asperger Publishing Company.

Wolfberg, P., O'Connor, T., Berry, R., & Fuge, G. (2001). *Combining integrated play groups and sensory integration: A unique approach for guiding peer interaction and play*. Autism Society of America, Millennium of Hope, National Conference on Autism. Arlington, TX: Future Horizons.